PYTHON MACHINE LEARNING

*Leveraging Python for Implementing
Machine Learning Algorithms and Applications
(2023 Guide)*

Roberta Bowman

First published by Roberta Bowman 2023

Copyright © 2023 by Roberta Bowman

All rights reserved. No part of this publication may be reproduced, stored or transmitted in any form or by any means, electronic, mechanical, photocopying, recording, scanning, or otherwise without written permission from the publisher. It is illegal to copy this book, post it to a website, or distribute it by any other means without permission.

First edition

This book was professionally typeset on Reedsy.
Find out more at reedsy.com

Contents

Introduction

Despite the recent explosion in machine learning, the truth is that we are still a long way from realizing its full potential. Currently, one of the hottest subjects in the IT industry is machine learning. The field of big data in particular is one on which you should concentrate all of your efforts since the potential is fantastic. The foundation of human existence in the not-too-distant future will be our connection with machines.

This book shows you how to use Python to construct machine learning methods, from the simplest to the most intricate. We covered a few Python packages designed expressly for machine learning in the earlier volumes of this series (Python for Beginners and Python for Data Analysis). We shall go into further detail in this volume to give a thorough grasp.

It's always a good idea to keep in mind the key machine-learning topics to concentrate on, even at advanced levels. The foundation of practically everything we do is an algorithm. For this reason, we've added a section where we'll briefly go over the most crucial algorithms as well as other helpful Machine Learning components.

Programming is a key component in machine learning, along with probability and statistics. We occasionally design optimal solutions in machine learning using a variety of statistical techniques. Therefore, in order to grasp the potential outcomes in each scenario, it is crucial to have a fundamental understanding of probability and statistics.

When exploring this subject, the idea that machine learning entails uncertainty frequently arises. One of the key distinctions between programming and machine learning is this. When you program, the code you create must be carried out exactly as it is written. Based on the supplied input, the code will produce a preset output. However, this is not a luxury we have in machine learning.

Learning, testing, and deployment are the three stages that must be taken into account in order to develop a Machine Learning model effectively. We can anticipate differences in the sort of interaction because models are typically created to interact with humans. For instance, it may be necessary to verify some inputs, in which case a suitable interaction will need to be built.

We also need to look at the mathematical component of machine learning as a field of research. Being an advanced level of study, we haven't covered it much in the series' earlier books. In order for the models to provide the output we require, machine learning involves a number of mathematical calculations. Because of this, we must learn how to manipulate the data in particular ways based on precise instructions.

There is always a potential that we will encounter large datasets when working with various datasets. This is typical since our machine learning models continue to learn and expand their expertise as they engage with other people. Utilizing large datasets might be difficult because you need to learn how to divide the data into manageable chunks that your system can easily process. This will also prevent your learning model from becoming overloaded.

When faced with enormous amounts of data, the majority of simple computers will fail. But once you know how to split up your datasets and do computations on them, this shouldn't be an issue.

We stated at the outset of this book that we will provide practical methods for utilizing machine learning in practical applications. In light of this, we examined some useful machine-learning techniques, including creating a spam filter and studying a movie library.

To make sure you can learn as you go, we have carefully broken down each step into its component parts. More significantly, we have attempted to explain each step so that you can better comprehend the actions you do and why.

The ultimate goal of creating a machine learning model is to integrate it into some of the everyday applications that consumers use. In light of this, you need to learn how to create a straightforward answer to this problem. We provided straightforward explanations to make sure you understood this, and as you continue working on various Machine Learning models, we hope that you will learn by creating increasingly complicated models that are tailored to your requirements.

Over time, you will learn or encounter a variety of machine learning principles. As long as your model interacts with data, you must remember that learning is an ongoing process. Greater datasets than the ones you are accustomed to dealing with will eventually come your way. Learning how to deal with them will enable you to do your tasks more quickly and painlessly.

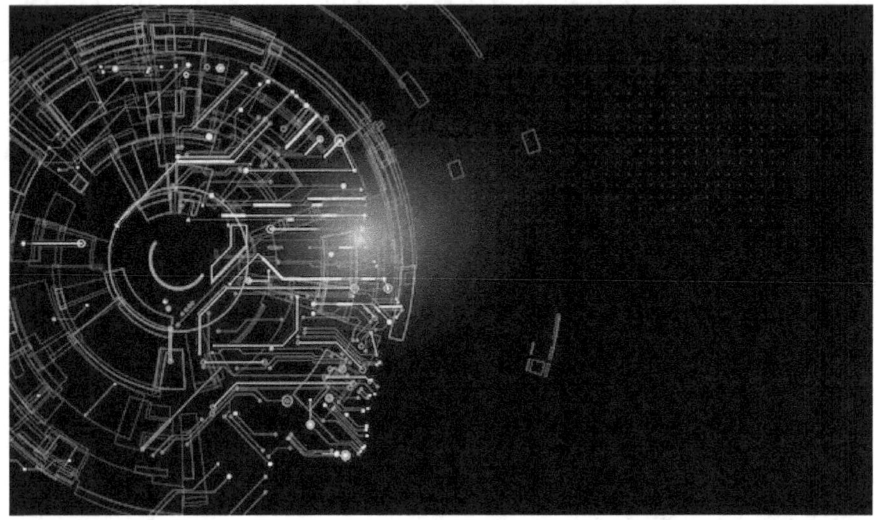

Chapter 1: What Is Machine Learning?

Technology has ingrained itself into our daily lives to such an extent that it cannot be separated from it. In fact, given how quickly technology is developing nowadays, artificially intelligent computers are now in charge of a variety of activities like prediction, recognition, diagnosis, and other things.

The input that must be supplied to machines in order for them to "learn" is represented by data. They are referred described as "training data" for this reason since they are utilized to teach the machines.

Once you've collected the data, you may examine it to look for any trends, and then take action based on those patterns. To assess the data and choose the best course of action, there are many learning methods. supervised learning and unsupervised learning are two categories into which these techniques might be divided.

There are many factors that make machine learning significant. As was already noted, all of the machine learning research is beneficial because it enables us to comprehend many facets of human learning. Additionally, machine learning is important since it improves the precision, potency, and efficacy of machines.

Here is a real-world illustration to assist you in better comprehending this idea.

Assume we have access to the music preferences of two unrelated users, A and B, who enjoy listening to music. A music label may use machine learning to determine the types of songs that each of these people enjoys and then consider the best ways to market to them.

For instance, you may examine several song characteristics like tempo, frequency, or voice gender before performing an analysis, possibly even graphically or visually. As more data is gathered, it will become clearer over time that, for instance, A tends to like fast-paced music with male singers, while B enjoys listening to calm songs with female singers, or any other trend.

comparable thought process. The marketing and advertising division of the business will be able to make wiser strategic decisions in light of these findings.

We currently have free access to a staggering amount of data that has been gathered since the development of technology. We can now store and process huge volumes of them, and they are open source. If you take a look at the way we can currently manage these things, technology has undoubtedly advanced. Today's technology is so advanced that it enables us to access ever-increasing amounts of data quickly.

Here are a few other arguments in favor of machine learning. There will always be some jobs that cannot be specified directly but only with the aid of examples, notwithstanding all the progress that is being made. The goal is to teach the machine to process data so that the output is independent of the input by first training it with data. By doing this, the machine will learn how similar inputs should be handled in the future and will handle them appropriately to get the desired results.

Additionally, it could be quite challenging to encode all the details a priori in the case of extremely complex operations. It is preferable in these situations for the machine to learn afterward from the output data of the process itself.

Data mining and machine learning are related fields. Data mining is the process of sifting through enormous amounts of data to identify patterns or connections. This is another advantage of machine learning because it enables computers to locate any data that can be of utmost significance.

Machine learning applications

The way businesses are conducted is significantly altering as a result of machine learning. It aids in the management of a sizable amount of data that is readily available and enables users to make helpful predictions in light of the available data.

When there is a lot of data involved, some manual operations cannot be finished quickly. The solution to these issues is machine learning. We are currently inundated with data and information, making the idea of manually processing it impossible.

As a result, there is a great demand for an automated approach, which machine learning aids with.

It is simpler to obtain valuable information when the analysis operations are entirely automated. This aids in totally automating all upcoming processes. Machine learning is necessary for the concepts of Big Data, Business Analytics, and Data Science. Now available to small firms and enterprises alike, predictive analytics and business intelligence are no longer just for high-end corporations. This makes it possible for small firms to participate in the successful information-gathering and use process. Let's examine a few technical Machine Learning applications and see how they relate to actual issues.

Personal digital assistants

Alexa, Siri, and Google Now are three common examples of virtual assistants that are now available. They assist the user in finding the required information via voice commands, as implied by the name. Simply turn it on and ask the query you want, such as "What is my schedule for the day?" Any additional inquiry you like, such as "What flights are available between London and Germany?"

Your personal assistant will research the matter, think back to the query you posed, and then respond to you. Additionally, it can be used to set reminders for particular tasks. Machine learning is crucial to the process since it makes it possible to

the system based on any of your prior interactions with it to compile and refine the information you require.

Systems of Recommendations

Machine learning algorithms built on probabilistic models can be used to generate suggestions for related products to users based on their purchasing history.

Just consider streaming services like Netflix or Amazon. With a considerable amount of past purchases, they surely have a strong understanding of their clients. They are able to accurately recommend the next item to purchase or movie to view as a result.

Latent Factors

To discover any association between the observed variables, latent variable models are used. When you are unsure about the connections between the variables, this is helpful.

To better understand the data, it is simpler to look for latent variables, especially when dealing with vast amounts of data.

Diminishment of Dimension

We frequently deal with data that has various variables and dimensions. For instance, weight, height, age, and blood pressure (in this case, four variables or dimensions) can be taken into account for a group of hospitalized patients. The data can be shown as a graph in 2D or 3D for two or three dimensions, connecting the different numerical data. The human mind cannot visualize the data in more than three dimensions.

There are methods for these circumstances that are made to handle fewer variables by reducing the number of variables that are present. The concept is straightforward: before applying any model, we analyze particular linear combinations of variables rather than all of them together.

Benefits and Drawbacks of Machine Learning

Disadvantages

Validating a machine learning model using a small dataset is one method for creating one. The objective is to forecast the output in relation to fresh data starting from a small dataset.

The issue with this method of operation is that it is challenging to determine whether the model produced has been distorted. For instance, the model can be overly dependent on the smaller dataset that was first utilized for model validation. Future conclusions might not be accurate as a result.

In the field of social sciences, machine learning has several applications. Given the foregoing, it is crucial to keep in mind that sometimes it may be required to enhance the models employed in order to prevent drawing incorrect conclusions.

Some of the benefits

Large amounts of data are impossible for humans to process, let alone analyze. There is a significant amount of real-time data being generated, and without an autonomous system to comprehend and evaluate that data, we are unable to draw any conclusions.

Machine learning is improving. The price of data engineering and pre-processing is decreasing with the introduction of Deep Learning algorithms.

Chapter 2: Terms and Concepts in Machine Learning

By providing the system with pertinent training data sets, machine learning is accomplished. Ordinary systems, or systems devoid of artificial intelligence, are always capable of producing an output based on the input received. However, a system with artificial intelligence may educate itself to learn, anticipate events, and enhance the outcomes it produces.

Let's take a look at a straightforward illustration of how kids discover what items are, or how they come to associate a word with an object. Assume that a dish of apples and oranges is there on the table. The round, red thing will be described as an apple by you, the adult or parent, and the orange by the other object. In this illustration, the qualities are the forms and colors, and the labels are the words "apple" and "orange." A set of labels and attributes can also be used to train a computer. Based on the inputted attributes, the machine will figure out how to identify the object.

Supervised Machine Learning models are those that are built using labeled training data sets. Children receive input about their progress from their teachers and professors while they are in school. Similarly to this, a supervised machine learning model enables the engineer to provide the machine with some feedback.

Take the input [red, round] as an example. Here, the child and the computer will both understand that an apple is any spherical, red thing. Now let's put a cricket ball in front of the machine or the kid, whichever you like. You can offer the machine feedback by rating it with 1 for right responses and 0 for incorrect responses. If you need more attributes, you can always add them. A machine can only learn in this manner. Additionally, because of this, if you utilize a sizable, high-quality data collection and devote more effort to training the

you will receive better and more accurate results from the equipment.

You must comprehend the distinctions between machine learning, artificial intelligence, and deep learning before we can move on. Although the majority of people confuse these ideas, it is crucial to understand that they are distinct.

A collection of methods and techniques known as artificial intelligence are utilized to make machines replicate any human behavior. The goal is to make sure that any human activity may be accurately and effectively mimicked by a machine. Deep Blue Chess and IBM's Watson are two instances of artificial intelligence-based technologies.

According to the definition given above, machine learning is the use of mathematical and statistical models to teach machines how to imitate human behavior. Data from the past is used for this.

As a subset of machine learning, deep learning refers to the tools and techniques an engineer uses to assist a computer in teaching itself. The device can learn to select the appropriate course of action to generate an output. The Deep Learning ecosystem includes Natural Language Processing and Neural Networks.

Machine learning's goals

One of the following is frequently a goal of machine learning.

- Decide on a category.
- Determine a quantity.
- Find anomalies
- Clustering

Decide on a category.

After analyzing the input data, the machine learning model forecasts which category the output will fall into. In these situations, the forecast is frequently a "yes" or "no" binary response. Examples of questions that will be feasible to answer include "Will it rain today or not?" "Is this a fruit?" and "Is this email spam or not?" and so forth. This is accomplished by making use of a set of data (training dataset) that determines whether or not a certain email qualifies as spam based on particular keywords. This method is referred to as classification.

Determine a quantity.

In this instance, the technique is typically used to forecast a value, such as the intensity of rainfall, based on various weather variables, such as temperature, humidity %, air pressure, and so on. Regression is the term used to describe this type of prediction. There are many subgroups of the regression method, including linear regression, multiple regression, etc.

Systems that Detect Anomalies

A model's job in anomaly detection is to find any outliers in the available data. In banking and e-commerce systems, where the system is designed to flag any anomalous transactions, these applications are employed. All of this aids in the detection of phony transactions.

Clustering

These technologies are still in their infancy, but they have a wide range of applications that have the potential to fundamentally alter how business is conducted.

For instance, it is feasible to organize people into several clusters based on various behavioral characteristics, such as their age group, the area they live in, or even the types of programs they prefer to watch. Because of this, businesses are now able to recommend various shows or programs based on the cluster to which the user belongs.

Machine Learning System Categories

In the case of conventional machines, the programmer will provide the machine with specific commands along with a set of instructions and input parameters, which the machine will utilize to perform computations and generate an output. However, with machine learning systems, the system is never constrained by any instruction that the programmer gives. The machine will select the algorithm that it can use to accurately process the dataset and determine the outcome. The training dataset, which comprises previous data and outputs, is used to accomplish this.

As a result, in the traditional world, we would provide a machine a set of instructions for how to process data, however in a machine learning setup, we would never give a system instructions. In order to produce an output, the computer must interact with the dataset, create an algorithm utilizing the historical data, make decisions similar to how a human would, and analyze the data. In contrast to a human, a computer can quickly process massive datasets and produce highly accurate findings.

Machine learning algorithms come in a variety of forms, and they are categorized according to their intended use. Machine learning systems fall into three categories:

1. Supervised Education
2. Unsupervised Education
3. Reward-Based Learning

Supervised education

These models feed labeled data into the computer. This is done in order to predict what particular datasets' (or new data's) results will be. Predictive algorithms are another name for this kind of algorithm.

Take the following table, for instance:

Money (label)
1USD
1EUR
1INR
1RU

Dimension (feature)
10 gm
5 gram
3 gm
7 gm

Each currency has a weight attribute in the table above. In this case, the weight is the property or feature, and the currency is the label.

With this training dataset as its first input, the supervised machine learning system will then predict that any input containing 3 grams is a coin weighing

1 INR. A 10-gram coin fits into the same category.

Algorithms for classification and regression analysis are within the category of supervised machine learning. While classification algorithms determine which category the data should fall under, regression techniques are used to forecast match results or home prices.

In the latter sections of the book, where we will also teach you how to construct or implement these algorithms using Python, we will go into more detail about a few of these algorithms.

Unsupervised Education

These models have a more sophisticated system since they can learn to find patterns in unlabeled data and generate an output. This type of approach is used to extract any significant inference from huge datasets. Since it uses data and summarizes it to create a description (or overview) of a given dataset, this model is also known as the descriptive model. Applications for data mining that require substantial amounts of unstructured input data frequently use this technique.

You can display the numerical data on a two-dimensional graph and perhaps spot clusters, for instance if the input data are names, runs, and wickets (the latter two being of a numeric kind). There will be two clusters in our scenario, one for the bowlers and one for the batsman. Additionally, it will be possible to associate a particular name with each point on the graph. When a new input will be available (provided by name, run, and wicket) can be linked to one of the two clusters to determine if the new input (player) is a bowler or a batsman.

The sample dataset for a match is in Table 1. This allows the cluster model to classify the players as bowlers or batters.

In unsupervised machine learning, popular algorithms including density estimation, clustering, data reduction, and compression are used.

The data are summarized and presented differently by the clustering method. This method is applied in data mining software. When the goal is to display any sizable data collection and produce an insightful summary, density estimation is performed. This will inevitably lead to the ideas of dimensionality and data reduction. These ideas clarify that the analysis or output must always provide a concise summary of the dataset without losing any important details. Simply said, if the derived result is valuable, the complexity of the data can be decreased.

The distinctions between supervised and unsupervised machine learning are outlined and summarized in the table below. Additionally, it will include the widely used algorithms of today.

We'll take a quick look at each of these algorithms and discover how to use Python to implement them.

Supervised Learning

- Works with labeled data
- Takes Direct feedback
- Predicts output based on input data. Therefore also called "Predictive Algorithm"

Some common classes of supervised algorithms include:

1. Logistic Regression
2. Linear Regression (Numeric prediction)
3. Polynomial Regression
4. Regression trees (Numeric prediction)
5. Gradient Descent

6. Random Forest
7. Decision Trees (classification)
8. K-Nearest Algorithm (classification)
9. Naive Bayes
10. Support Vector Machines

Unsupervised Learning

- Works with unlabeled data
- No feedback loop
- Finds the hidden structure/pattern from input data. Sometimes called as "Descriptive Model"

Some common classes of unsupervised algorithms include:

1. Clustering, Compressing, density estimation & data
2. Reduction
3. K-means Clustering (Clustering)
4. Association Rules (Pattern Detection)
5. Singular Value
6. Decomposition
7. Fuzzy Means
8. Partial Least Squares
9. Hierarchical Clustering
10. Principal Component Analysis

Reinforced education

In that the system will learn how to behave in a particular environment and take actions based on that environment, this form of learning is comparable to how humans learn. Humans, for instance, avoid touching fire because they are aware that it will hurt and have been told that it will harm them. We may occasionally stick our fingers into a fire out of curiosity and discover that it will burn. This indicates that going forward, we'll exercise caution around the fire.

Now let's look at some real-world applications of machine learning. It is wise to know what kind of machine you are dealing with.

You must employ an instructional model with examples. Later in the book, the examples below will be covered in further detail:

Face-recognition software for Facebook

Recommendations for shows on Netflix or YouTube based on previous viewing habits

examining a huge number of financial transactions to determine whether they are legitimate or fraudulent.

The surge pricing model for Uber

Building a Machine Learning System:

Steps

Here are the typical processes that are involved in creating a machine learning system, regardless of the model being used.

Describe the Goal

The first step, as with anything in life, is to identify your goals. Knowing what you hope to achieve with your system is crucial. The type of prediction you want the system to make will determine the type of data you use, the algorithm, and other variables.

1. Gather Information

Perhaps the longest step in the development of a machine learning system is this one. To prepare the algorithm for use, you must gather all the pertinent data.

Prepare the data in 2.

This is a crucial step that is frequently skipped. Ignoring this step could end up costing you money. The output will be more accurate the cleaner and the more pertinent the data you are using.

3. Choose a Method

You can select from a variety of algorithms, including Structured Vector Machine (SVM), k-mean, Naive-Bayes, Apriori, etc. The algorithm you choose will mostly depend on the goal you want the model to help you achieve.

4. Develop Your Model

Once all the data are prepared, the machine must be fed with them so that the algorithm may be trained to forecast.

5. Examine the Model.

Your model is now prepared to start reading the input and producing the desired outputs when it has been trained.

6. Foresee

The algorithm will go through several iterations, and you may also give it input to help it make better predictions over time.

7. Send out

The model will be sanitized and ready for integration into any application when you test it and are satisfied with how it performs. This indicates that it is prepared for deployment.

Depending on the application and the kind of algorithm (supervised or unsupervised) you're employing, all these phases can change. They do, however, participate in every step of creating a machine learning system. Each of these levels allows you to employ a variety of languages and technologies. This book teaches us how to use Python to create a machine-learning system. Let's examine the examples from the preceding section:

Scenario No. 1

Facebook detects a friend's image in a photo from a tagged album.

This is an illustration of supervised learning. Facebook in this instance is using tagged images to identify the person. The images' labels will be created from the tagged images. Supervised learning is the process through which a computer learns from any type of labeled data.

Scenario No. 2

fresh song recommendations based on listener history.

This is an illustration of supervised learning. The music genre is one of the pre-existing or categorized labels that the model is being trained on. Exactly this is what Netflix, Pandora, and Spotify do: they compile the music and movies you enjoy, assess the qualities based on your preferences, and then recommend songs and movies based on features that are comparable.

Scenario No. 3

to identify any questionable or fraudulent transactions by analyzing bank data.

This is an illustration of unsupervised learning. There are no explicit classifications like "fraud" or "not a fraud" in this instance because the suspicious transaction cannot be completely specified. The model will look for abnormal transactions in an effort to spot any outliers.

Scenario No. 4

the cost of an Uber ride, which fluctuates according to the time of day that you utilize the service.

Explanation: The Uber surge pricing function combines several machine learning models, such as the forecast of peak hours, traffic in particular areas, and the availability of cabs. The usage patterns of people in different parts of the city are identified using clustering.

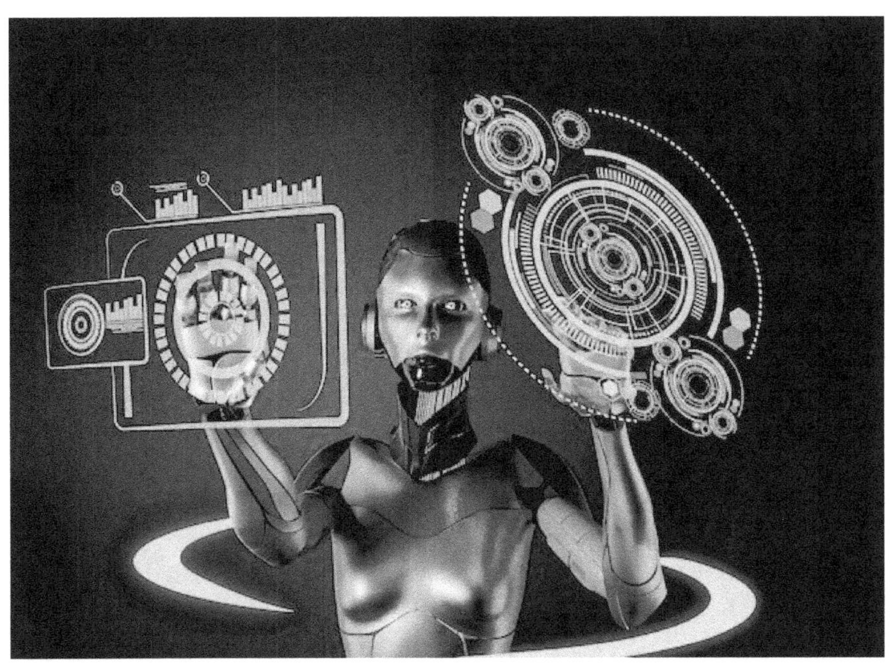

Chapter 3: Essential Libraries for Machine Learning in Python

Today, Python is frequently chosen by developers to examine data. Python is useful for more than just data analysis; it may also be used to develop statistical techniques. Python is preferred by everyone who works with data for data integration. That is how Web applications and other environment-based creations are integrated.

Python's features have made it possible for researchers to use it for machine learning. Its advantages include having a consistent syntax, being adaptable, and even taking less time to create. Additionally, it contains engines that could aid with forecasts and the ability to create intricate models.

Python thus claims of having a number or collection of very comprehensive libraries. Recall that libraries relate to a collection of procedures and various types of functions written in various languages. So having a strong library can help you take on activities that are more challenging. This can be done, though, without having to repeat numerous lines of code. It's important to remember that machine learning heavily relies on mathematics. Specifically, mathematical optimization along with aspects of statistics and probability. Python is therefore incredibly helpful for completing complicated jobs quickly.

The libraries listed below are a few of the more well-known ones.

Scikit-Learn

One of the top and most popular libraries for machine learning is Scikit Learn. It is capable of assisting learning algorithms, particularly supervised ones. It is used for a variety of algorithms, including the following:

- k-means
- Tree decisions
- Logistic and linear regression
- Clustering

Major parts of this type of library come from SciPy and NumPy. In addition to performing tasks connected to data mining, Scikit-learn provides the ability to add algorithm sets that are helpful in machine learning. It aids in categorization, clustering, and even regression analysis, that's all. Additionally, there are other jobs that this library can effectively complete. Ensemble methods, feature selection, data transformation, and other techniques are good examples. It's important to realize that the advanced and complex elements of algorithms can be simply implemented by specialists.

TensorFlow

In order to do computations quickly, Google produced the TensorFlow library, which is widely used in the deep learning industry. It enables computations to be done on a CPU or GPU. That is, once you create the code in Python, your computer will be able to execute it. Because of this, analysis is carried out relatively quickly.

TensorFlow uses nodes, which allow for the processing of a significant amount of data, to carry out various activities within the system. This library is a prerequisite for numerous search engines like Google. Speech recognition and object identification are a couple of crucial applications.

Theano

Another important Python library is Theano. Its primary responsibilities are to assist with anything involving numerical computation. It's also comparable to NumPy. It also performs additional jobs, such

- An explanation of mathematical terms
- Mathematical calculation optimization
- Evaluating numerical analysis-related phrases.

Theano's major objective is to produce effective results. Due to its ability to multiply calculations involving large amounts of data by 100, it is a speedier Python package. So it's important to know that Theano performs better on a GPU than a computer's CPU. People utilize Theano for deep learning across various industries. Additionally, they compute intricate and difficult jobs using it. Its processing speed made all of this feasible. Many individuals utilize the most recent version of this library because companies with a high need for data computation techniques are expanding. Keep in mind that the most recent one first gained attention years ago. Theano's latest version included a number of enhancements, interface tweaks, and new features.

Pandas

A very well-liked library called Pandas aids in the provision of high-level, high-quality data structures. These are straightforward, user-friendly statistics. It makes sense in this situation as well. It is made up of a variety of complex internal techniques that enable it to carry out operations including grouping and timing analysis. It also aids in the combining of data and provides filtering options, which is another function. Pandas may gather information from additional sources, including SQL databases, Excel, and CSV files. In order to carry out its operational tasks inside the industries, it can also change the data that has been acquired. Pandas are made up of two structures that allow them to correctly carry out their functions. These are data frames with two dimensions and series with just one dimension. Over time, the Pandas library has been considered the most reliable and potent Python library. Its primary purpose is to facilitate data manipulation. Additionally, it includes the ability to import and export a variety of data. It has uses in a variety of industries, including data science.

The following areas are where Pandas excels:

- Dividing up data
- Data combining two or more types
- Aggregation of data
- Choosing or adjusting data
- Reshaping data

You can swiftly add new texts to the data frame or fast delete specific columns. It will support data conversion for you.

You can feel confident that Pandas will find any lost or missing data.

It has a strong ability, especially when it comes to organizing other programs into functional groups.

Matplotlib

Another powerful and practical library, particularly for data visualization. It was created with the intention of giving many sectors practical and visual insights. A company's accomplishments in business, for instance, don't make much sense if you can't communicate them to various stakeholders. For anyone working with data visualization, Matplotlib is a vital Python package with a large range of possibilities. This library is excellent for graphics and photos. It is adaptable, just needs a few keystrokes, and enables you to create any type of chart you would desire, including histograms, scatterplots, non-Cartesian charts, etc.

It is important to note that this library can export graphics and convert them to PDF, GIF, and other formats. In conclusion, the following tasks are quite simple to complete. They consist of:

- Development of line plots
- Dispersion of plots
- Amazing bar chart creations and histogram construction
- Numerous pie charts are used in the industry.
- Stemming the Data Analysis and Computational Schemes
- The ability to monitor contour plots
- Using spectrograms
- Quiver plans to create

Using diagrams to explain

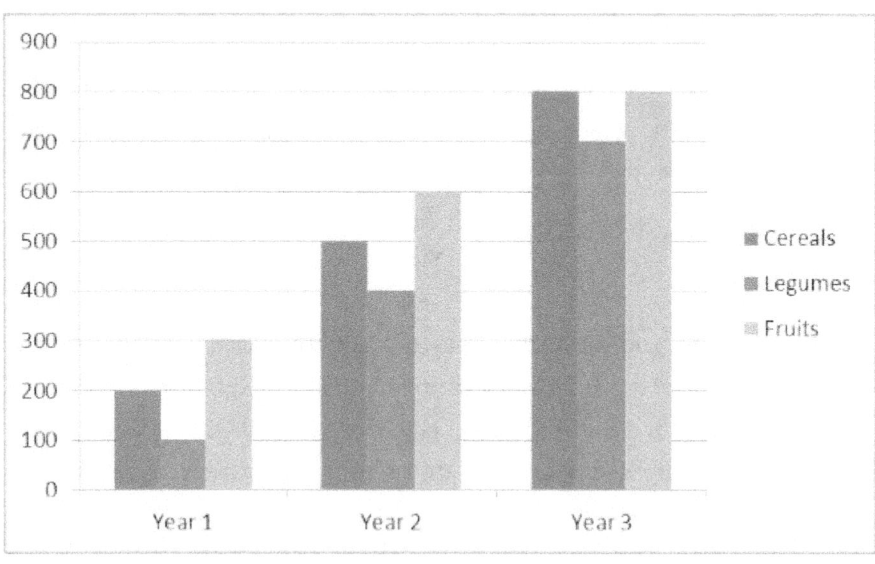

The production of an organization during a three-year period is seen in the graph above. It notably shows how Matplotlib is used for data analysis. You can see from the diagram that production was higher than it was in the previous two years. Once more, the business consistently outperforms in the production of fruits as it did in years 1 and 2 with a tie in year 3. You can see from the figure that using this library has made your job with presentation, representation, and even analysis easier. You will soon be able to create high-quality graphic graphics, correct statistics, and much more with the help of this Python package. You will be able to record the year in which your production was high, allowing you to continue the period of high productivity.

Here's another illustration:

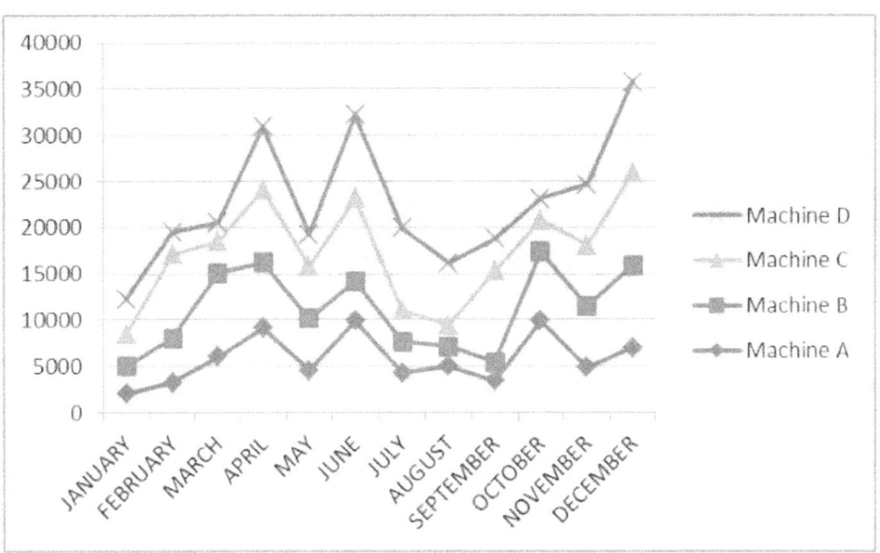

The performance of the many computers the organization uses is clearly displayed in the above line graph. You can eventually determine and draw a conclusion on which machines the business can maintain using to achieve the maximum yield by using the diagram above. You can typically forecast the precise capabilities of your various inputs using this evaluation method and the Seaborn library. Once more, this information can be useful for future research should you decide to buy additional computers. The Seaborn library also provides the capability to gauge the effectiveness of additional variable inputs within the

company. For instance, the number of employees inside the organization and their related working rate can be simply determined.

Seaborn

One of the most well-liked Python libraries is Seaborn. Its primary goal in this instance is to aid in visualization. It's vital to remember that Matplotlib served as the foundation for this library. Because of its higher level, it is able to generate a variety of plots, including time series plots and heat maps, as well as process violin graphs.

NumPy

This Python library is quite popular. It can process multidimensional arrays thanks to its features. Additionally, it supports matrix processing. These, however, can only be achieved with the aid of a wide range of mathematical functions. It is vital to mention that the most significant computations within the scientific field can be solved very well using this Python module. Once more, NumPy has applications in areas including Fourier transformation, linear algebra, and the development of random number capabilities utilized in various industries. Other sophisticated Python libraries, such as TensorFlow, employ NumPy for manipulating Tensors. NumPy's primary uses are computation and data storage, to put it briefly. Python may also be used to export or load data because it offers the features necessary to carry out these tasks. The fact that this Python package is also referred to as numerical Python is also important to note.

SciPy

SciPy boasts of having a variety of modules that can be used in data analysis optimization. In addition, it is crucial in the areas of integration, linear algebra, and other mathematical statistics.

It frequently plays a crucial part in image alteration. Image manipulation is a technique that is frequently used in day-to-day activities. SciPy uses cases from Photoshop and many other applications. Again, a lot of businesses like SciPy for image modification, especially when it comes to images for presentations. A wildlife club might, for instance, create a description of a cat and then alter it with various colors to fit its purpose. You can grasp this more simply by using the example below. The image has been altered:

The wildlife society took a picture of a cat for the original contribution. We obtain a colored image of a cat after manipulating and resizing the image to suit our needs.

Keras

This is a fundamental component of the Python library, particularly when it comes to machine learning. It is a member of the class of highly neural networks. It is important to remember that Keras may operate over other libraries, including TensorFlow and even Theano. It can also run continuously without any mechanical issues. Additionally, it appears to perform better on the CPU and GPU. For the majority of Python programming newcomers, Keras provides a safe path to complete comprehension. They will have the ability to create the network from scratch. It is considered the greatest Python library among beginners since it allows for quicker and more efficient prototyping.

PyTorch

Another open-source, user-friendly Python library is this one. Because of its name, it claims of offering a wide range of tool options. It is also applicable in fields where computer vision is available. Visual display and computer vision are crucial components of many different kinds of study. It assists with the processing of Natural Language once more. Additionally, PyTorch is capable of performing several developer-specific technical tasks. That involves a lot of mathematics and Data Analysis. It can aid in the production of graphs, which are mostly utilized for computational purposes. It can operate on other libraries like Tensors because it is an open-source Python library. Its acceleration will rise when combined with Tensors GPU.

Scrapy

Another library for crawling programs is called Scrapy. That includes spider bots and a lot more. The utilization of spider bots is frequently utilized for data retrieval and for creating URLs that are used on the internet. Its original purpose was to aid with data scraping. However, this has undergone a number of changes that have increased its broad purpose. As a result, the primary function of the Scrapy library in the modern period is to serve as a general-purpose crawler. The library encouraged widespread use and the use of global codes, among other things.

Statsmodels

A library called Statsmodels was created with the purpose of exploring data using various statistical computing and assertion techniques. It contains numerous features, including distinguishing attributes and result data. It can carry out this function using a variety of models, including linear regression, multiple estimators, time series analysis, and even more linear models. Also suitable are other models, including discrete choice.

We will delve deeply into the TensorFlow Library in this chapter. This is an additional Python option that is very beneficial for carrying out specific Machine Learning operations more quickly. Then, learning how to use this option in conjunction with the methods we discussed using the Scikit-Learn package is absolutely time well spent.

TensorFlow provides programmers with a variety of capabilities and tools to help them finish projects more quickly. When trying to work on various models linked to deep learning, you'll discover that the framework that comes with TensorFlow is from Google and is useful. For numerical computing, TensorFlow will rely on graphs of data flow, and it can ensure that some of the various things you can accomplish with machine learning are simpler than before.

We will benefit from TensorFlow in a variety of ways. In the beginning, it can assist us in gathering the data, training the machine learning models that we are attempting to employ, making forecasts, and even modifying some of the upcoming outcomes that we have to make them function more effectively. We can see how TensorFlow can enter our project and ensure we attain that completion that we desire even better as each of these processes will be crucial when it comes to implementing some machine learning.

Let's first examine TensorFlow and some of the background information that comes with this Python package. TensorFlow was first created by the Google Brain team for use in large-scale machine learning options. It was created to combine various Deep Learning and Machine Learning techniques and will increase the utility of such algorithms by using a "common metaphor." The Python programming language, which we previously discussed, is compatible with TensorFlow. Additionally, it will give consumers access to a front-end API that they can easily utilize when working on various building applications.

But it goes a little bit beyond. Even if you can use TensorFlow and it is compatible with the Python programming language as you code and creates your algorithms, it will have the ability to alter these. The C++ programming language will be used to run every application you use with TensorFlow, providing them with an even greater level of performance than before.

TensorFlow can be used for a wide range of tasks that are necessary for a successful machine-learning project. Running, training, and developing deep neural networks, performing image recognition, dealing with recurrent neural networks, digit classification, natural language processing, and even word embedding are some of the things you can accomplish with this library. And these are just a handful of the things a programmer can do when they use TensorFlow in conjunction with machine learning.

TensorFlow installation

In light of this, before utilizing this library, we must spend some time learning how to set up TensorFlow on a computer. We must go through and set up the environment and everything else so that this library will function, just like we did with Scikit-Learn. You will appreciate that with this kind of library because it is already going to be set up with a few programming APIs, like Rust, Go, C++, and Java, to mention a few (we will look at these in more detail later). The TensorFlow library will be examined in this article's focus on the Windows operating system, but the procedures you must follow to add this library to other operating systems will largely be the same.

There are now two options available for you to choose from when you are ready to install and download the TensorFlow library on your Windows machine. A pip will also work well, or you may choose to use the Anaconda program to do the task. The native pip is useful since it ensures that the TensorFlow library is installed on your system by gathering all of the components that go with it. Additionally, the system performs this task for you without requiring a virtual environment to be set up.

Although it can appear to be the greatest option, there may be issues along the way. While using pip to install the TensorFlow library can be quicker and doesn't require a virtual environment, there may be some conflict with other Python tasks. This could be a problem depending on what you intend to achieve using Python, so take that into account before you begin.

The good news in this situation is that you can get the entire TensorFlow library to run with just one command if you decide to work with a pip and it doesn't appear to be going to interfere with what you are doing too much. And once you've finished running this command, the entire library and all of its components will be set up and available for use with simply a single command on the computer. Additionally, pip makes it simpler for you to select the location where you want to store the TensorFlow library for quicker access.

You can use the Anaconda program in addition to the pip to aid in downloading and installing the TensorFlow library. This one will require a few more commands to get going, but it does stop any Python program interference from occurring and allows you to create a virtual environment that you can work in and test out without experiencing a lot of interference or other problems with what is on your computer.

Despite the fact that there are a few advantages to utilizing the Anaconda program rather than a pip, it is frequently advised that you install this software alongside a pip rather than using the conda install alone. In light of this, we'll still walk you through some of the procedures necessary to use the conda install by itself if you choose.

Before continuing on, there is one more item that has to be taken into account: make sure that the Python version is operational. For this to work for you, your Python version must be 3.5 or higher. The pip 3 tool, which is used by Python 3, is the best and most compatible one when it comes to interacting with a TensorFlow installation. When using a previous version of this library, your machine-learning code may not run as smoothly and may experience other problems.

Depending on the version of this library you are most comfortable with, you can use either the CPU or the GPU. The CPU version is represented by the first code below, and the GPU version is represented by the second code below.

Installing pip 3 and upgrading TensorFlow

Installing pip 3 and upgrading tensorflow-gpu

These two actions are advantageous since they will make sure that the TensorFlow library is set up on your Windows PC. However, you also have the Anaconda package itself as an alternative. The aforementioned techniques were still effective.

Despite the fact that there are certain disadvantages with the pip installs, we discussed them.

When you install Python on your machine, Pip is the program that is already pre-installed. However, you might learn very quickly that Anaconda is not. This means that you must first install the Anaconda program if you want to make sure that TensorFlow can be installed with this. Simply visit the Anaconda website and then adhere to the on-screen directions to complete this.

Once you've had a chance to install the Anaconda program, you'll see that there is going to be a package called conda in the files. This package is useful to look into a little bit right now because it will help you manage the installation packages and will be useful when it comes time to administer the virtual environment. You may simply set up Anaconda to assist you acquire the access you require with this package.

When Anaconda is running, go to the Windows start screen, click the Start button, and then select All Programs. To view the files inside of Anaconda, you must navigate through and expand items. You may then select the Anaconda prompt to open it on your screen by clicking on it. If you'd like, you may open the command line and type "conda info" to view this package's details. This enables you to see some additional information about the package and the package management that you require.

The virtual environment we discuss with the Anaconda software will be quite easy to use and is essentially simply a standalone version of Python. It will be equipped with all the tools you need to manage all the files you use, as well as the directories and paths that go along with them. This is advantageous since it enables you to complete all of your coding within the Python application and, if you so want, to incorporate additional Python-related libraries.

These virtual environments might take some getting used to, but they are useful for working on machine learning because they let you focus on one project at a time and allow you to code without worrying about dependencies or version requirements. You won't mess with other portions of the code because everything you do in the virtual environment will run on its own, allowing you to experiment and observe what works and what doesn't.

The next step is to use the Anaconda program to set up the desired virtual environment, which will enable the TensorFlow package to function as intended. To accomplish this, the conda command will be used once more. We will need to give it the name tensorenviron as we are currently going through the procedures required to establish a completely new environment. The remaining syntax will then help us create this new environment, and it contains the following:

Tensor Environment: conda construct -n

The application will halt when you enter this code into the compiler and prompt you to choose whether you wish to construct the new environment or if you would prefer to stop what you are doing right now. We're going to type the "y" key here, hit enter, and the environment will be established. As the compiler sets up the environment for you, the installation process could take a little while.

Once the new environment has been built, you must go through the activation process. You won't have the environment set up for you without this activation. To begin, you only need to execute the "activate" command, followed by a list of the names of any environments you want to work with. You should use the name "tensorenviron" in your code since we already used it. An illustration of how this will seem is as follows:

Turn on tensorenviron

After successfully activating the TensorFlow environment, it is now time to ensure that the TensorFlow package will also be deployed. The following command can be used to accomplish this:

install tensorflow with conda

When you reach this stage, a list of all the packages that are available to install will be shown to you in case you want to include a few extras in addition to TensorFlow. After that, you may choose whether to install one or more of these packages or to continue using TensorFlow for the time being. As soon as you agree to do this, make sure to move through with the process.

This library's installation will start working immediately. However, it will be a lengthy process, so just let it continue without attempting to backspace or start over. Your internet's speed will play a significant role in determining whether or not this will take a lengthy time.

But as soon as the installation of this library is complete, you can check to see if everything went smoothly or if there are any issues that need to be fixed. The good news is that since Python's import statement can be used to set up the checking step, working with it will be simple.

The standard Python terminal will then be used to execute the statement that we are writing. You would be able to press enter after inputting the word Python if you were still working here as you should be with Anaconda's prompt. By doing this, you can be sure that you are in the Python terminal you need to get started. Once you are at the appropriate terminal, enter the following code to assist us and ensure that TensorFlow is imported and ready to use:

tf import tensorflow

The program should now be installed and ready to use on your computer, so we can continue with the rest of the manual and look at some

What you can accomplish with this library is one of the cool things. There's a potential that the TensorFlow package didn't process correctly in the end. If this is the case for you, the compiler will issue an error notice for you to review, and you must go back and double-check that the code was written in the proper format at each step.

The good news is that if you complete the above line of code and receive no error message at all, this indicates that you have correctly configured the TensorFlow package and it is ready for use! Now that we know how to use the TensorFlow library, let's investigate some additional options and algorithms that a programmer can use to learn how they interact with the various Machine Learning projects you want to use them in.

Chapter 4: Machine Learning Training Model

A model in machine learning is a logical or digital representation of an actual procedure. The correct training data must be given to an algorithm by developers in order for it to create a strong Machine Learning (ML) model. On the other hand, an algorithm is a hypothetical set that is taken before training with real-world data starts.

For instance, a linear regression algorithm is a collection of functions that define traits or qualities that are similar to those specified by linear regression. From a set or group of functions, developers select the function that best fits the majority of the training data. Giving an algorithm training data is a necessary step in the machine learning training process.

Any machine learning model should be created with the basic intention of exposing it to a large amount of input and any relevant output so that it may analyze it and utilize to understand how it relates to the outcomes. For instance, a person would need to consider the weather conditions, which in this case would be the training data, in order to decide whether or not to take an umbrella depending on the weather.

Professional data scientists devote more time and energy to the procedures that come before the following processes:

1. Data investigation
2. Cleaning of data
3. Developing fresh features

Python Simple Machine Learning Training Model

Having the appropriate data is more crucial for machine learning than being able to create complex algorithms. Effective modeling will minimize over-fitting and maximize performance. Data are a finite resource in machine learning, and developers should use them to:

- Training their model or feeding their algorithm

- Validating their model.

They cannot, however, carry out both tasks using the same data. If they did this, they might over-fit their model without even realizing it. Because a model's efficiency depends on its capacity to anticipate previously unobserved or novel data, it is crucial to have distinct training and testing datasets. Utilizing training sets is primarily intended to fit and optimize a model. On the other hand, test sets are fresh datasets used to assess a model.

To obtain the most accurate estimations of the model's performance, data must first be separated. Until one is prepared to select the final model, one should refrain from touching the test sets after completing this. The ability to compare training and test performance enables developers to prevent over-fitting. When a model performs well on training data but poorly on test data, this indicates that the model has a performance issue.

Over-fitting is one of the most crucial issues in the field of machine learning. It explains how well the provided training data correlates with the target function's approximation. It occurs when there is a high signal-to-noise ratio in the training data, which will produce inaccurate predictions.

In essence, an ML model is overfitting if it generalizes new data badly while fitting the training data remarkably well. To solve this issue, developers add a penalty to the model's parameters, which restricts the model's freedom.

Professionals typically refer to modifying hyper-parameters when they discuss fine-tuning machine learning models. Model parameters and hyper-parameters are the two primary categories of parameters in machine learning. Decision tree locations and regression coefficients are examples of the first category, which defines specific models and is a learned attribute.

However, the second kind specifies more advanced parameters for machine learning algorithms, such as the size of the penalty applied by regression algorithms or the number of trees in a random forest method.

Giving an algorithm training data is the first step in training a machine-learning model. The model artifact produced by the ML training process is referred to as a machine-learning model. The desired property, or the correct response, should be included in this data. The algorithm searches for data patterns that indicate the outcome it wants to anticipate and builds a model that incorporates these various patterns.

When making predictions on fresh data, developers might apply machine learning models even while they are unaware of the target features. For example, if a developer wanted to train a model to determine if an email is real or spam, he or she would provide it with training data that included emails that had labels that indicated whether the emails were authentic or not. The model will attempt to predict if a new email is real or spam by using this data to train it.

Linear regression is used in a simple Python machine-learning model.

Beginners need to download and install sci-kit-learn, an open-source Python library with a wide range of visualization, cross-validation, pre-processing, and Machine Learning algorithms utilizing a uniform user interface, in order to develop a basic ML model in Python. It provides straightforward features that can be used to save a lot of time and effort. Additionally, developers' computers must have Python Version 3 installed.

The following are some of sci-kit-learn's key characteristics:

1. Effective and user-friendly Data Analysis and Data Mining tools BSD license 2.
2. Highly useable and accessible, and may be reused in several scenarios
3. Built upon the SciPy, NumPy, and Matplotlib foundations
4. Companion job functionality
5. Outstanding documentation
6. Using appropriate defaults when adjusting settings
7. A user interface that supports different ML models

It is necessary for users to have SciPy and NumPy installed prior to installing this library. They must separate an existing data collection into training, testing, and validation data if it already exists. In this instance, however, they are building their own training set that will include both the input and desired output values of the data set they intend to utilize to train their model. They can utilize the Panda package, which makes it simple to load and modify datasets, to load an external dataset.

As an example, a = N = b. Their input data will be made up of random integer values that will produce a random integer N. As a result, they will develop a function to establish the output. Remember that a function returns an output value based on an input value. They will divide each row into an input training when they have created their training set.

two lists of all inputs and their matching outputs are produced from the training set and its associated output training set.

The following advantages of partitioning datasets:

1. Increasing the model's ability to be trained and tested on data types other than those used for training
2. checking the model's precision, which is preferable to check the out-of-sample training's precision
3. The capacity to assess predictions using test dataset response values

They will then build and train their model, which will attempt to replicate the function they developed for the ML training dataset, using the linear regression approach from Python's sci-kit-learn module. They must now decide whether their model can replicate the intended function and produce the right response or precise forecast.

The machine learning (ML) model examines the training data in this case and uses it to determine the coefficients or weights to apply to the inputs in order to produce the desired outputs. The model will yield an accurate result if given the proper test data.

Chapter 5: Linear Regression with Python

One-variable linear regression

We will first concentrate on the case in which there is just one variable in linear regression. This will make things a little bit simpler to deal with and ensure that we can master some of the fundamentals before attempting some of the more challenging tasks. We'll concentrate on issues with just one independent variable and one dependent variable.

We will utilize the data set for car_price.csv to get started on this one so that we can determine what the price of the vehicle will be. The cost of the car will serve as our dependent variable, and the year of the car will serve as our independent variable. These files are located in the Data sets directories that we previously discussed. We will need to use the Scikit Learn package from Python to help us find the correct linear regression technique so that we can produce an accurate forecast about the cost of the autos. Once everything is set up, we need to employ the next several procedures to assist.

Bringing in the proper libraries

To begin, we must confirm that we have the appropriate libraries on hand. The following codes are required to obtain the libraries for this section:

bring in pandas as pets

import np for Numpy

import plt from matplotlib.pyplot

inline %matplotlib

This script can be used in a Jupyter Notebook. If you're using the Jupyter Notebook, the final line must be present; however, if you're using Spyder, you can omit the final line since Spyder will process and complete this step on its own.

Bringing the dataset in

The next stage will be importing the data sets you want to employ for this training method after the libraries have been imported using the codes you already had. We'll use the dataset "car_price.csv" for our task. To assist you in placing the data set correctly, you can run the script below:

car_data is equal to pd.read_csv("D:Datasetscar_price.csv").

studying the information

It is always better to practice and examine the data for any scaling or missing value issues before using the data to aid in training. We must first look at the information. The first five rows of the data set that you want to display will be returned by the head method. To make this one work, you can use the script below:

car_data.head()

Additionally, you can get all of the dataset's statistical details back via the described function.

describe_car_data ()

Let's look at the linear regression procedure one last time to determine if it will work for this kind of activity. The data points will be taken and plotted on the graph. This will enable us to determine whether the price and the year are related. Use the script below to test whether this will succeed:

car_data['Year'], car_data['Price'] plt.scatter

"Year vs. Price" in plt.title

plt.xlabel("Year")

plt.ylabel("Price")

plt.show()

When we employ the aforementioned script, we are attempting to deal with a scatterplot that we can later locate on the Matplotlib package. This will be helpful because the year will be on the x-axis of the scatter plot and the price will be over on the y-axis. We can see from the output figure that the price of the car will climb in tandem with an increase in the year. This demonstrates the existence of a linear link between

the price and the year. This is a useful example of how this kind of method might be applied to address the issue at hand.

Relating to data preparation

Now that we have that knowledge, we need to use it to accomplish these two tasks. You must use the script below to begin dividing the data into features and labels:

characteristics are equal to car_data.iloc[:,0:1].values

labels equal to car_data.iloc[:,1].values

Since there are just two columns here, the feature set will be in the 0th column, and the label will be in the first. The data can then be split in half, with 20% going to the training set and the rest going to the test set. Use the scripts listed below to assist you in completing this:

import train_test_split train_features, test_features, and train_labels from sklearn.model_selection.

(Features, labels, test_size = 0.2, random_state = 0), test_labels = train_test_split

We can go back and review the data set after this section. When we do this, it is simple to see that there won't be a significant discrepancy between the values of the prices and the years. These two will ultimately cost hundreds of dollars each. This means that you can use the data as it is right now without the need for any scaling. In the long term, that saves you some time and work.

How to program the algorithm to predict certain events

It's time to train the algorithm a little bit so that it can provide accurate forecasts for you. The LinearRegression class will be useful in this situation as it has all the labels and other training features you'll need to enter and train your models.

You just need to follow the script below to get started, and it's easy to do:

import from sklearn.linear_model LinearRegression() with the argument lin_reg

.eatures, train_labels) lin_reg.fit

We will check the coefficient for just the independent variable using the same example of automobile prices and the prior years. To do it, we must employ the script that follows:

print(lin_reg.coef_)

This technique will produce the number 204.815 as a result. This demonstrates that the car price will rise by 204.815 (at least in this example) with every change in units during the year.

Predicting the new instance that you will work with is the last step to perform after spending the time to train this model. To make this happen, the anticipated method will be applied to this kind of class. The approach will use the test features you select as an input and then forecast the output that most closely resembles that input. The script that you may use to accomplish this is as follows:

predictions are equal to lin_reg.predict(test_features).

When you use this script, you'll discover that it's going to accurately anticipate what the future holds for us. Based on the information we now have, we can make an educated judgment as to how much a car will be worth depending on the year it is built in the future. Future changes might affect some things, and it does appear to impact based on the features that come with the automobile. However, this is a useful approach to have a look at the cars and get a general idea of how much they currently cost and how much they will cost moving forward.

So, let's check out how this functions. Now that we have examined this linear regression, we want to determine how much a car will cost us in 2025. Perhaps you're planning to save money for a car and want to know how much it will cost you once you have that money. You could utilize the details we provided.

Have the new year that you want it to be based on, add it in, and then calculate the typical price of a new car for that year.

Naturally, keep in mind that this won't be entirely correct. Prices may change as a result of inflation, and the manufacturer may make changes as well. There will be greater and lower prices from time to time. However, it at least provides you with a reliable method of estimating the cost of the car you already own and how much it will cost you in the future.

Chapter 6: Neural Networks

The essential feature of artificial and convolutional neural networks is covered in this chapter. It also discusses their constituent parts, in particular the activation functions, how artificial neural networks are trained, as well as the various benefits of employing them.

Artificial Neural Network Definition

A common strategy in machine learning is the deployment of artificial neural networks. It takes its cues from the human brain. Neural networks aim to imitate the way the human brain learns. The neural network system consists of input, output, and a hidden layer that converts data from the input layer into information that is helpful to the output layer. Typically, an artificial neural network has numerous hidden layers. An illustration of a neural network system with two hidden layers is shown in the image below:

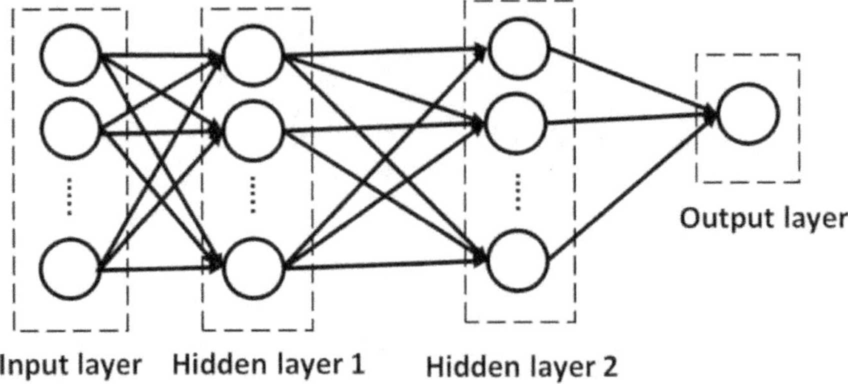

Example of an artificial neural network

Before going further and explaining how Neural Networks work, let's first define what a neuron is. A neuron is simply a mathematical equation expressed as the sum of the weighted inputs. Let's consider

$$X = \{x_1, x_2, ...,x_M\}$$

A vector of M inputs, the neuron is a linear combination of all inputs defined as follows:

$$F(X = \{x_1, x_2, ...,x_M\}) = w_1x_1 + w_2x_2 + \ ... \ + w_Mx_M$$

being the weights assigned to each input. The function F can also be represented as:

$$F(X) = WX$$

Where W is a weight matrix and X a vector of data. The second formulation is very convenient when programming a neural network model. The weights are determined during the training procedure. Training an artificial neural network means finding the optimal weights W that provide the most accurate output.

To each neuron, an activation function is applied the resulted weighted sum of inputs X. The role of the activation function is deciding whether the neuron should be activated or not according to the model's prediction. This process is applied to each layer of the network. In the following sub-sections, we will discuss in detail the role and types of activation functions as well as the different types of Neural Networks.

What is the purpose of an activation function in neural network models?

Mathematical functions are used to formulate activation functions. A model of an artificial neural network must have these features. An activation function is connected to every neuron. The decision to activate the neuron or not is made by the activation function. For illustration, have a look at what a neuron produces, which is:

$$Y = \sum weight \times input + bias$$

Any value may be the output Y. The reasonable range of values that Y can have is not known to the neuron. In order to accomplish this, the activation function has been incorporated into the neural network to evaluate Y values and determine whether or not the neural connections should regard this neuron as activated.

Different activation functions come in various forms. The step function is the most natural function. If a specific threshold is exceeded, this function determines whether or not to activate a neuron. In other words, if Y exceeds a certain threshold, this function returns 1; otherwise, it returns 0. The activation function is official:

$$F = \begin{cases} 1, & \text{if } Y > \text{threshold} \\ 0, & \text{otherwise} \end{cases}$$

where 1 denotes activation and 0 denotes inactivation.

For a classification issue where the output should be yes or no (i.e., 1 or 0), this activation function can be employed. But it has several shortcomings. Let's take a collection of possible input categories (such as class1, class2,..., etc.) as an example. The output will be 1 for all neurons if this activation function is utilized when more than one neuron is activated. Because all neuron outputs in this scenario are 1, it is challenging to distinguish between the classes and determine which class the input belongs to. In other words, the step function does not permit classification into multiple classes or numerous output values.

In contrast to the step function, the linear activation function offers a variety of activation values. The output is computed to be proportional to the input. Formally:

$$F(X) = WX$$

where the input is X.

Instead of only supporting 1 or 0, this function also accepts multiple outputs. This function does not allow backpropagation for model training because it is linear. Backpropagation is a method for updating the parameters, in particular the weights, by using a function derivative or gradient. The linear activation function's derivative, or gradient, has a fixed value of W and is unaffected by changes in the input X. As a result, it does not disclose which weights applied to the input can produce reliable predictions.

Additionally, when applying the linear function, all layers can be condensed into a single layer. The last layer is a linear function of the first layer due to the fact that all layers use a linear function. As a result, using more than one layer in a neural network serves no use because they are all equivalent to the first layer. The intricacy of the input data cannot be supported by a linear regression model, which is what a neural network with numerous layers coupled by a linear activation function is.

Because relationships between the output and the input features are typically non-linear in real-world applications, the majority of neural networks employ non-linear activation functions. The irregular

The neural network's functionalities enable it to map intricate patterns between inputs and outputs. Additionally, they enable the neural network to learn the intricate procedures governing complicated or high dimension input, including images and audio, among others. The limitations of step functions and linear functions can be overcome by using non-linear functions. They permit stacking several layers (i.e., the combination of non-linear functions is non-linear) and backpropagation (i.e., the derivative is not a constant and depends on the changes of the input). A neural network can employ a variety of non-linear functions. The most popular non-linear activation functions in machine learning applications will be covered in this book.

Sigmoid Operation

One of the most popular activation functions in an artificial neural network is the sigmoid function. Formally, a sigmoid function is equal to the product of the exponential of the inputs and the inverse of the sum of one:

$$F(X) = \frac{1}{1 + \exp(-X)}$$

A sigmoid function's outputs have a range between 0 and 1. The outputs, to be more specific, take any value between 0 and 1 and offer precise predictions. In fact, the value of Y is close to the curve's edge (i.e., closer to 0 or 1) when the X is bigger than 2 or lower than -2.

The drawback of this activation function is the minimal change in output for input values, as shown in the figure above.

to a maximum of 4. The term "vanishing gradient" refers to an issue when the gradient is very minimal on the horizontal extrema of the curve. As a result, sigmoid neural networks learn relatively slowly as they get closer to the edges and are computationally expensive.

The tanh process

Another activation function that is employed that is comparable to the sigmoid function is the tanh function. This function's mathematical description is as follows:

$$F(X) = \tanh(X) = \frac{2}{1 + \exp(-2X)} - 1$$

The scaled sigmoid function describes this function. As a result, it shares the sigmoid function's properties. The gradient of this function is more prominent than the gradient of the sigmoid function, although its outputs span from -1 to 1. The tanh function is zero-centered, unlike the sigmoid function, which makes it ideal for inputs with negative, neutral, and positive values. Similar to the sigmoid function, this function has the problem of vanishing gradients and is computationally expensive.

The ReLu feature

Another popular and effective activation function is the Rectified Linear Unit function, sometimes referred to as the ReLu function. Compared to the sigmoid and tanh functions, this function is effective and enables the neural network to converge fast. This is due to the fact that it uses straightforward mathematical formulations. If X is positive, ReLu outputs X; else, 0 is returned. This activation function is described in formal terms as

$$F(X) = \max(0, X)$$

This activation function accepts values between 0 and +inf and is not bounded. The ReLu function has a derivative even though it resembles a linear function in shape (i.e., this function equals zero for positive values). The ReLu has the flaw that when the inputs are negative, the derivative (i.e., the gradient) is 0. This indicates that the backpropagation cannot be processed for linear functions.

and without inputs greater than 0, the neural network cannot learn. The dying ReLu problem refers to the ReLu feature where the gradient is equal to 0 when the inputs are negative.

Two ReLu variants, the Leaky ReLu function, and the Parametric ReLu function, can be utilized to avoid the dying ReLu problem. The maximum of X and X by 0.1 is the output of the Leakey ReLu function. In other words, when X is greater than 0, the leaky ReLu equals the identity function, and when X is lower than 0, it equals the product of 0.1 and X. The following service is offered:

$$F(X) = \max(0.1X, X)$$

This function supports backpropagation for negative values since it has a tiny positive gradient (0.1) when X contains negative values. It might not, however, offer a reliable forecast for these negative values.

The Leaky ReLu function, which uses the gradient as a parameter to the neural network to define the output when X is negative, is comparable to the parametric ReLu function. This function's mathematical description is as follows:

$$F(X) = \max(aX, X)$$

The exponential linear ReLu function is one of several versions of the ReLu function. The log curve for negative values of X is used in this function rather than the linear curves used in the Leaky ReLu and the parametric ReLu functions, which are the other two versions of the ReLu. This function's drawback is that it saturates for very large negative values of X. There are more variations that share the fundamental idea of defining a gradient as larger than zero when X has negative values.

The Softmax component

A different kind of activation function than the one just described is the Softmax function. When it's necessary to divide the inputs into numerous classes, this function is often only applied to the output layer. In fact, the Softmax function offers the likelihood of input to multiple classes and supports belong to a certain group. To calculate the likelihood, it first normalizes the outputs of each category between 0 and 1, then divides them by the sum of those outputs.

Which of these activation functions, each of which has advantages and disadvantages, should be applied to a neural network? The response is that especially if the properties of the function being approximated are known beforehand, merely having a better understanding of the problem at hand will help direct into a certain activation function. For a classification issue, a sigmoid function is an excellent option. It is strongly advised to start with a ReLu function rather than attempting alternative activation functions if the type of the function being approximated is uncertain. Overall, a variety of applications benefit from the ReLu feature. You could use your activation function to participate in the ongoing research.

The sparsity of the activation is a crucial consideration when selecting an activation function. Not all neurons are activated in a sparse population. This is a beneficial feature in a neural network since it speeds up learning and reduces the risk of overfitting. Imagine a vast neural network with many neurons, all of which are processed to describe the output if all of them are triggered. Because of this, processing the neural network requires a lot of computation. Since practically all neurons are activated by the sigmoid and tanh activation functions, they are computationally less effective than the ReLu function and its variants, which inactivate some negative values. Because of this, it is advised to begin by approximating a function with known features using the ReLu function.

What different kinds of artificial neural networks are there?

There are numerous types of artificial neural networks, each with unique characteristics and levels of complexity. The perceptron is the earliest and most basic neural network ever created. The output layer receives the result from the perceptron after it has added up the inputs and applied an activation function.

The feedforward neural network is another dated and straightforward method. There is only one layer in this particular artificial neural network type. It is a category that has complete connectivity to the layer below, where each node is connected to every other node. Through the hidden layer, it propagates information in a single way from the inputs to the outputs. The front propagating wave, which often employs the activation function, is the technical term for this phenomenon. Each layer's node's data is processed by this activation function. This neural network outputs a weighted sum of the inputs computed using the activation function of the hidden layer. The backpropagation method and the logistic function are typically used in feedforward neural network training and activation, respectively.

This kind of network is a derived type of several other Neural Networks. The radial-basis-function Neural Networks, as an illustration. With this feedforward neural network, the logistic function is replaced by the radial basis function. This kind of neural network contains two layers, the inner layer of which combines the radial basis function with the features. Each point's distance from the relative center is calculated using the radial function. For calculating the distance from the target value for continuous variables, this neural network is helpful.

The logistic function, in contrast, is used to map any binary value, such as yes or no (0 or 1). A multilayer feedforward neural network is a deep feedforward network. Since they produce better results, they have become the most often utilized type of neural network in machine learning. From these varieties of Neural Networks, a brand-new learning paradigm known as Deep Learning has developed.

Another category that employs various node types is recurrent neural networks. Each hidden layer processes the information for the subsequent layer, much like a feedforward neural network. Outputs from concealed layers are nonetheless saved and processed back to the top layer. The input layer's first layer is processed as the product of the weighted features added together. The recurrent process is used in layers that are not visible. Every node will save data from the preceding phase at each step. While the computation is underway, memory is used. In order to enhance the predictions, the recurrent neural network uses forward propagation and backpropagation to self-learn from the prior time steps. In contrast to feedforward neural networks, information is processed in two ways here.

A neural network with three or more layers is known as a multilayer perceptron or multilayer neural network. Every node in this group of networks is connected to every other node in the layers below, making them fully connected.

Convolutional neural networks are frequently helpful for classifying or identifying images. This particular artificial neural network's processing is made to handle pixel data. Convolutions, which operate as filters for neuron activation, are the foundation of multi-layer convolutional neural networks. The same feature is activated when the same filter is applied to a neuron, creating what is known as a feature map. The strength and significance of a feature in the input data are reflected in the feature map.

Multiple connected neural networks combine to build modular neural networks. These networks rely on the "divide and conquer" strategy. They are useful for solving extremely complicated issues because they let different kinds of neural networks be combined. As a result, they enable the combination of the advantages of several neural networks to address complicated problems where each neural network is capable of handling a particular task.

An Artificial Neural Network's training procedure

Neural networks compute a weighted total of inputs and apply an activation function at each layer, as was stated at the beginning of this chapter. The output layer is then given the end result. Forward propagation is a frequent name for this process. Weights must be tuned in order to create the most accurate outputs when training these artificial neural networks. The following steps are involved in training an artificial neural network:

1. Set the weights at zero

2. Use the process of forward propagation
3. Assess the effectiveness of the neural network
4. Use the backward propagation technique
5. Refresh the weights
6. Continue with steps 2 through 6 until the maximum number of iterations is reached or neural network performance is not enhanced.

We need a performance metric that defines how accurate the neural network is, as we can see from the procedures of training an artificial neural network that was previously described. The loss function or cost function is the name of this function. The cost function we discussed in the previous chapter could be the same as this function:

$$J = \frac{1}{N}\sum(y_{predicted} - y_{target})^2$$

where is the output, N is the number of outputs, and is the output's actual value. The neural network error is provided by this function. The neural network's great accuracy is reflected by small values of J.

We have thus far described loss function and the general operation of neural networks. Let's now discuss each stage of the training process in more depth.

Let's think about a group of X inputs and Y outputs. We start out with a null matrix for W (the weights) and B (the bias). Applying the feed-forward propagation, which entails feeding each layer of data with a

the artificial neural network's bias and input weights added together. Think about the fact that there are two layers. The output of the first hidden layer can be calculated using the equation below:

$$Z_1 = W_1 X + b_1$$

Where W1 and b1 are the neural network's parameters for the first layer's weights and bias, respectively.

The activation function F1, which can be any activation from the function previously discussed in this chapter, is then applied.

$$A_1 = F_1(Z_1)$$

The output of the first layer is the final product, which is then fed to the second layer as follows:

$$Z_2 = W_2 A_1 + b_2$$

The second layer's weights and bias are represented by W2 and b2, respectively.

We then use an activation function F2 to this outcome:

$$A_2 = F_2(Z_2)$$

The artificial neural network's output is now meant to be A2. Depending on the dataset and the desired result, the activation functions F1 and F2 may have the same activation function or be separate activation functions.

Following feedforward propagation, we use the loss function to compare the neural network output to the desired output. At this point, there is a very good chance that the discrepancy between the estimated output and the actual data is substantial. As a result, we must modify the weights using the backpropagation method. With regard to biases and weights, we calculate the gradient of each activation function. Prior to assessing the derivative of the input layer, we first evaluate the derivative of the previous layer. The weights should then be updated based on the gradient or derivative of the activation function. Applying these methods to our two-layer neural network example yields the following results:

$$W_2 = W_2 - \alpha \frac{d}{dW} F_2(W,b) \qquad b_2 = b_2 - \alpha \frac{d}{db} F_2(W,b)$$

$$W_1 = W_1 - \alpha \frac{d}{dW} F_2(W,b) \qquad b_1 = b_1 - \alpha \frac{d}{db} F_2(W,b)$$

The learning rate parameter is the parameter. The weights' update frequency is determined by this parameter. The gradient descent algorithm is the name of the procedure we just described. The procedure is repeated until the predetermined maximum number of iterations has been reached. In Chapter 4, using Python, we will construct an example to demonstrate a perceptron and multi-layer neural network. A classifier based on an artificial neural network will be created. Let's now look at the benefits of applying artificial neural networks to machine learning applications.

Use of artificial neural networks: advantages and disadvantages

Artificial neural networks are used today practically everywhere. Numerous artificial neural networks have emerged to fully utilize this Artificial Intelligence methodology as a result of the intense research activity in this field. Artificial neural networks offer a number of benefits.

Structures can be mapped by artificial neural networks, which can also learn from data more quickly. Additionally, as is the case in many real-world applications, they are able to map the intricate linkages and structures that link the output datasets to the input datasets. An artificial neural network can be generalized after it has been created and trained. In other words, it may be used to predict outcomes for new datasets or map associations between data that it hasn't been exposed to. Furthermore, there are no presumptions about the distribution or structure of the input data made by the artificial neural network. Unlike conventional statistical methods, it does not place restrictions on the data or make assumptions about how the data are related. Artificial Neural Networks are a useful tool since they can process a lot of data. Artificial neural networks are a non-parametric method that enables model development with a reduced error that is brought on by parameter estimation. Artificial neural networks have certain appealing qualities, but they also have some disadvantages.

Artificial neural networks have the drawback of frequently operating in the dark. As a result, we are unable to properly comprehend the connection between inputs and outputs as well as the interdependence between particular input variables and the output. In other words, we are unable to quantify the influence of each input variable on the outcome. Computationally, the training procedure may be inefficient. By employing parallel computing and making effective use of the computing capacity of computers, we may solve this issue.

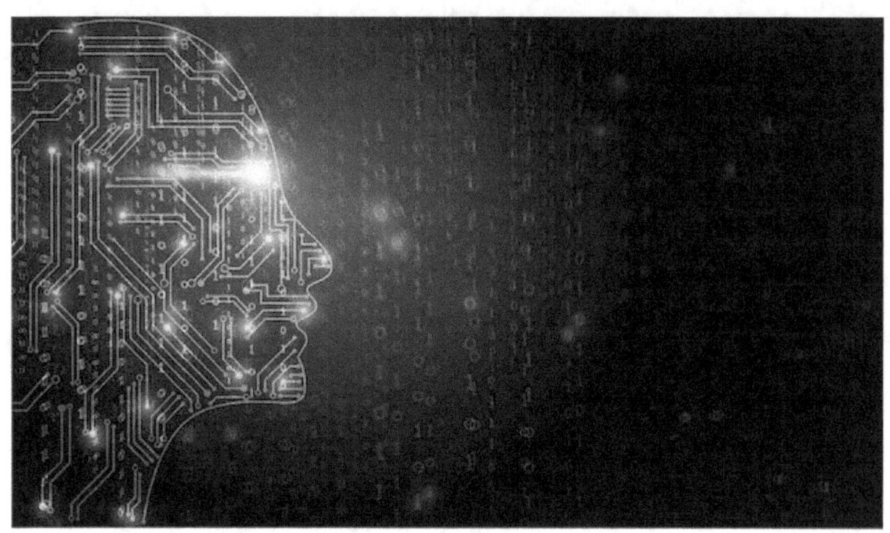

Chapter 7: Neural Networks With Convolutions

Convolutional Neural Networks (CNNs) are one of the main types of deep neural networks that have demonstrated excellent performance in a wide range of computer science fields, including object recognition, object classification, and computer vision. ConvNets have been used for many years to separate different faces, identify objects, and power robot and self-driving car vision systems.

A ConvNet can quickly identify numerous photographic sequences and offer pertinent caption suggestions. ConvNets can also recognize commonplace items, animals, or people. Convolutional neural networks have recently been successfully used for NLP issues like sentence classification.

Convolutional Neural Networks are therefore among the most crucial tools for Deep Learning and machine learning applications. LeNet was the first Convolutional Neural Network to be introduced, and it considerably advanced the Deep Learning field as a whole. Yann LeCun first suggested this type of convolutional neural network in 1988. It was mostly used to solve character recognition issues like reading codes and numerals.

This first Convolutional Neural Network proposed back in 1988 is extremely similar to Convolutional Neural Networks that are frequently used nowadays for numerous computer science tasks.

LeNet was employed for a variety of character recognition applications, just like modern convolutional neural networks. Similar to LeNet, the commonly used convolutional neural networks have four basic operations: classification of their fully-connected layers, sub-sampling or pooling, ReLU non-linearity activation functions, and convolution.

Every Convolutional Neural Network is constructed using these operations as their cornerstones. We must delve further into these four fundamental functions in order to move on to working with convolutional neural networks in Python and gain a better knowledge of the logic that underlies convolutional neural networks.

Every image, as you are aware, may be simply represented as a matrix with various values. When referring to a particular aspect of photographs, we will use the common word "channel." Commonly, an image produced by a conventional camera has three channels: blue, red, and green. These pictures can be thought of as three stacked two-dimensional matrices. Additionally, each of these matrices has specified pixel values between 0 and 255.

However, since there are only black and white pixels in a grayscale image, there is only one channel available. The sample we are examining is only a single-2D matrix that depicts a grayscale image because, in this situation, we are just going to be thinking about grayscale images. Each pixel in the matrix must have a value between 0 and 255. In this instance, 0 denotes a black color whereas 255 denotes a white hue.

Convolutional Neural Networks: Their Operation

For many Deep Learning issues, a Convolutional Neural Network structure is typically employed. Convolutional Neural Networks are employed for object recognition, object segmentation, detection, and computer vision because of their structure, as was already established. CNNs do not require the manual feature extraction that is frequently necessary for conventional deep neural networks because they learn directly from the picture input.

There are three key reasons why CNN usage has increased in popularity. The first of these is the structure of CNNs, which does away with the requirement for manual data extraction because all data features are directly learned by CNNs. The second reason CNNs are becoming more and more well-liked is that they deliver outstanding, cutting-edge results for object recognition. The final justification is that CNNs can be readily kept around to help create other deep neural networks for a variety of new object detection jobs.

A CNN may have hundreds of layers, each of which automatically learns to recognize a variety of features in visual input. The output of every convolved picture is used as the input to the next convolutional layer since filters are frequently applied to every training image at various resolutions.

As the convolutional layers advance, the filters can also start with relatively basic picture properties like edges and brightness and then gradually enhance the complexity of those image attributes, which define the object.

Since the output of each convolved image serves as the input for the subsequent convolutional layer, filters are frequently applied to each training image at various resolutions.

Convolutional neural networks can be trained using millions, tens of thousands, or even only a few hundred photos.

Use GPUs that can handle enormous volumes of image data and intricate network architecture when you're doing this.

may greatly reduce the amount of time needed to process data when training a neural network model.

Once your convolutional neural network model has been trained, you may utilize it for a variety of real-time tasks, including object recognition and pedestrian detection in ADAS, or advanced driver assistance systems.

The output layer is the final fully connected layer in a standard deep neural network, and it represents the overall class score in every classification setting.

These characteristics prevent standard deep neural networks from scaling to complete images. For instance, all of the images in CIFAR-10 are 32x32x3 in size. This indicates that all CIFAR-10 images have three color channels and are 32 inches wide and high. In a first conventional neural network, this implies that a single fully-connected neural network would have 32x32x3 or 3071 weights. Given that those fully-connected structures cannot scale to larger images, this amount is not as manageable.

In order to swiftly add up additional parameters, you would also like to have more neurons that are comparable. However, using fully-connected neurons in this situation of computer vision and other problems of a similar kind is inefficient as your parameters will fast lead to over-fitting of your model. Convolutional Neural Networks, which are used to solve these kinds of Deep Learning challenges, benefit from the fact that their inputs are images.

Convolutional Neural Networks restrict the architecture of images in a much more logical way because of their structure. Convolutional Neural Network layers are made up of neurons that are arranged in three dimensions, encompassing depth, height, and breadth, unlike layers in a typical deep neural network. For instance, the input volume of all layers in a deep neural network includes the CIFAR-10 input images, and the volume has the size 32x32x3.

Instead of all the layers being totally connected, the neurons in these types of layers can only be connected to a tiny portion of the layer preceding it.

connected in the same way as typical deep neural networks. The output of the final layers for CIFAR-10 would also have 1x1x10 dimensions because the design of the convolutional neural networks has reduced the entire image to a vector of a class score by the time it was finished, arranging it only along the depth dimension.

To sum up, a ConvNet assembles all of its neurons in just three dimensions, in contrast to conventional three-layer deep neural networks. Each layer in a convolutional neural network also converts the 3D input volume into a 3D output volume that contains different neuron activations.

An output volume with a 3D differentiable function and layers with simple APIs are produced by a convolutional neural network, which may or may not include neural network parameters.

Convolutional layers, sometimes followed by fully-connected or dense layers, are the building blocks of a convolutional neural network. As you are already aware, the input of a convolutional neural network is an image with dimensions of n x n x r, where n stands for the input picture's height and breadth and r for the total number of channels. Additionally, k filters known as kernels may be present in convolutional neural networks. When kernels are present, their q value—which may be equal to the number of channels—is determined.

Each Convolutional Neural Network map is subsampled using a maximum or means pooling method over p x p of a continuous area, where p typically varies between 2 and 5 depending on the size of the image. Every feature map is given a sigmoidal non-linearity and additive bias either after or before the subsampling layer. There may be a number of fully-connected layers following these convolutional neural layers, and the structure of these fully-connected layers is the same as that of conventional multilayer neural networks.

Padding and Stepping

Second, you must provide the stride that you slide over the filter in addition to the depth. You can only move one pixel at a time while your stride is one. When your stride is two, you can move two pixels at once, however this results in lower spatial output volumes. The stride value is one by default. However, if you want to find less overlap between your receptive fields, you can make larger strides. However, as was already noted, this will lead to smaller feature maps because you are skipping over image spots.

When using larger strides but still wanting to keep the same number of dimensions, you must employ padding, which encircles your input with zeros. You have two options for padding: zeros or values at the edge. When your feature map's dimensionality matches your input, you can proceed to add pooling layers, which are widely employed in convolutional neural networks to maintain the size of feature maps.

Your feature maps will get smaller as you add more layers if you don't employ padding. When you wish to pad your input volume with nothing but zeros all the way around the border, adding zero padding might be very useful.

Zero-padding is the name of the hyperparameter for this. You can manage the size of your output volumes by utilizing zero padding.

The size of your input volume, the convolution layer's receptive field, the stride you applied, and the amount of zero-padding you employed in your convolutional neural network boundary can all be utilized to simply calculate the spatial size of your output volume.

For instance, if you apply a 3x3 filter with stride 1 and pad 0, you will obtain a 5x5 output if your input is 7x7. The formula is as follows, where W stands for the size of your input volume, F for the receptive field size of your convolutional neural layers, S for the applied stride, and P for the quantity of zero-padding you used. If you have stride two, you will get a 3x3 output volume, and so on.

$$(W-F+2P)/S+1$$

You can quickly determine how many neurons will fit in your convolutional neural network by using this formula. When possible, think about utilizing zero padding. For instance, you can utilize zero-padding of one to get three receptive fields provided your input and output dimensions are equal, which is five.

In situations like this, if you do not employ zero-padding, your output volume will have a spatial dimension of 3, as there are three neurons that can fit in your original input.

Mutual constraints are a typical feature of spatial arrangement hypermeters. Stride cannot be applied, for example, if your input size is 10, you don't utilize zero-padding, and your filter size is 3. In order to make the set of your hyperparameters valid, your Convolutional Neural Networks library will either throw an exception or totally zero pad the remaining values.

Fortunately, any task may be made simpler by correctly scaling the convolutional layers so that all included dimensions operate using zero padding.

Sharing Parametrics

You may completely regulate the number of used parameters by using parameter-sharing strategies in your convolutional layers. You can force the neurons contained in each depth slice to utilize the same bias and weights if you designate a single two-dimensional slice of depth as your depth slice. One of every depth slice will be obtained using parameter-sharing procedures, and you will also obtain a unique set of weights. As a result, you can greatly minimize the number of parameters in the ConvNet's first layer.

By completing this step, your ConvNet's neurons in every depth slice will use the same settings.

In other words, each neuron in the volume will autonomously calculate the gradient for each of its weights during backpropagation.

You only need to update one collection of weights per depth slice because these computed gradients will accumulate throughout all depth slices. By doing this, the weight vector for each neuron in a depth slice will be the same. As a result, the forward pass of the convolutional layers is computed as a convolution of the input volume and weights from all neurons for each depth slice. For this reason, the set of weights we obtain—which is convolved with your input—is referred to as a kernel or filter.

However, there are some situations in which the assumption of parameter sharing is absurd. This is frequently the case when there are numerous input images to a convolutional layer that has a specific centered structure; in this situation, you must learn various characteristics depending on the location of your image.

For instance, you would anticipate receiving various hair- or eye-specific traits when you have an input of several faces that have been centered in your image. These properties could be easily learned at numerous spatial positions. It is fairly typical to just loosen this parameter-sharing technique and employ a locally-connected layer in these circumstances.

Multiplication of Matrix

These dot products between the local input regions and the filters are frequently carried out via the convolution process. In these circumstances, one typical method of convolutional layer implementation is to make full use of this feature and formulate the primary convolutional layer's forward passed as a single massive matrix multiply.

When the local regions of an input image are entirely extended out into various columns during the procedure known as im2col, matrix multiplication is implemented. For instance, if your input is 227x227x3 and your filter is 11x11x3 with a stride of 4, you must extract blocks of pixels from the input that are 11x11x3 and extend each one into a column vector that is 363 pixels wide.

However, if you repeat this process with a 4-stride input, you will have 55 locations, along with weight and height, which will result in an output matrix with x columns, each of which has a maximally stretched-out receptive field and a total of 3025 fields.

Your input volume's numbers can be repeated in numerous separate columns. Also, keep in mind that the convolutional layer weights are similarly stretched out into certain rows. For instance, if you have 95 filters that are each 11 by 11 by 3, you will obtain a matrix with w rows and a 96 by 363 dimension.

When it comes to matrix multiplications, the output of your dot production of every filter at every location will be the same as the result of performing one massive matrix multiply that evaluates the dot products between every receptive field and between every filter. When you have your desired outcome, you must reformat it to fit the desired output dimension, in this example 55x55x96.

Although this strategy is excellent, there is a drawback. Due to several replications of the values in your input volume, the biggest drawback is that it consumes a lot of memory. However, the primary advantage of

Multiple matrix multiplication implementations can enhance your model. In addition, when you conduct a pooling operation, this im2col can be used repeatedly.

Conclusion

I appreciate you continuing to read.

When it comes to all of these needs and more, Python Machine Learning might be the solution you're looking for. Your computer may be taught to learn on its own using a straightforward procedure, far quicker and more effectively than the human mind can. This manual attempted to outline the precise measures you can follow to achieve this, as it has changed the game in many industries.

When it comes to employing Machine Learning in their code, a programmer can accomplish so much, and when you combine it with the Python coding language, you can take it even further, even as a newbie.

The following step is to begin using some of the knowledge that we covered in this manual. When it comes to machine learning, there are many fantastic things you can do, and when we mix it with the Python programming language, there is nothing we can't accomplish when it comes to training our machine or computer.

This manual took its time to examine a variety of the possibilities offered by Python machine learning. We examined the basics of machine learning, and how to use it, and even received a crash lesson in utilizing the Python programming language for the first time. Once that was finished, we immediately began integrating the two of them to use a number of Python libraries to complete the task.

This manual is the ultimate tool you need if you've ever wanted to learn how to use the Python coding language or explore what Machine Learning can accomplish for you. Consider reading it to learn more about Python Machine Learning's potential for you.